I0410873

Congressional
Research Service
Informing the legislative debate since 1914 _____

SBA Veterans Assistance Programs:
An Analysis of Contemporary Issues

Robert Jay Dilger
Senior Specialist in American National Government

Sean Lowry
Analyst in Public Finance

October 23, 2014

Congressional Research Service

7-5700

www.crs.gov

R42695

Summary

Several federal agencies, including the Small Business Administration (SBA), provide training and other assistance to veterans seeking civilian employment. For example, the Department of Defense, in cooperation with the Department of Labor, Department of Veterans Affairs, and several other federal agencies, including the SBA, operates the Transition Goals Plans Success program (Transition GPS), which provides employment information and entrepreneurship training to exiting military servicemembers to assist them in transitioning from the military to the civilian labor force.

In recent years, the SBA has focused increased attention on meeting the needs of veteran small business owners and veterans interested in starting a small business. In FY2013, the SBA provided management and technical assistance services to more than 100,000 veterans through its various management and technical assistance training partners (e.g., Small Business Development Centers, Women's Business Centers [WBCs], Service Corps of Retired Executives [SCORE], and Veterans Business Outreach Centers [VBOCs]). In addition, the SBA's Office of Veterans Business Development (OVBD) administers several programs to assist veteran-owned small businesses.

Congressional interest in the SBA's veteran assistance programs has increased in recent years primarily due to reports by veteran organizations that veterans were experiencing difficulty accessing the SBA's programs. Congress also has a continuing interest in assisting veterans, especially those returning from overseas in recent years, in their transition from military into civilian life. Although the unemployment rate (as of September 2014) among veterans (4.7%) was lower than for nonveterans aged 18 years and older (5.7%), the unemployment rate of veterans who have left the military since September 2001 (6.2%) was higher than the unemployment rate for nonveterans.

The expansion of federal employment training programs targeted at specific populations, such as women and veterans, has also led some Members and organizations to ask if these programs should be consolidated. In their view, eliminating program duplication among federal business assistance programs across federal agencies, and within the SBA, would result in lower costs and improved services. Others argue that keeping these business assistance programs separate enables them to offer services that match the unique needs of various underserved populations, such as veterans. In their view, instead of considering program consolidation as a policy option, the focus should be on improving communication and cooperation among the federal agencies providing assistance to entrepreneurs.

This report opens with an examination of the current economic circumstances of veteran-owned businesses drawn from the Bureau of the Census's 2007 Survey of Business Owners, which was administered in 2008 and 2009 and released on May 17, 2011. It then provides a brief overview of veterans' employment experiences, comparing unemployment and labor force participation rates for veterans, veterans who have left the military since September 2001, and nonveterans. The report describes the employment assistance programs offered by several federal agencies to assist veterans in their transition from the military to the civilian labor force and examines, in greater detail, the SBA's veteran business development programs, the SBA's efforts to assist veterans' access to capital, and the SBA's veteran contracting programs. It also discusses the SBA's Military Reservist Economic Injury Disaster Loan program.

Contents

Tables

Contacts

SBA Assistance for Veterans

The Small Business Administration (SBA) administers several programs to support small business owners and prospective entrepreneurs. For example, it provides access to entrepreneurial education programs to assist with business formation and expansion; loan guaranty programs to enhance small business owners' access to capital; and programs to increase small business opportunities in federal contracting, including oversight of the service-disabled veteran-owned small business federal procurement goaling program.[1] The SBA also provides direct loans for owners of businesses of all sizes, homeowners, and renters to assist their recovery from natural disasters.

One of the SBA's disaster loan programs, the Military Reservist Economic Injury Disaster Loan (MREIDL) program, is of particular interest to veterans. The MREIDL program provides disaster assistance in the form of direct loans of up to $2 million to help small business owners who are not able to obtain credit elsewhere meet ordinary and necessary operating expenses that they could have met but are not able to because an essential employee has been called up to active duty in his or her role as a military reservist or member of the National Guard due to a period of military conflict.[2]

In FY2013, the SBA provided management and technical assistance services to more than 100,000 veterans through its various management and technical assistance training partners (e.g., Small Business Development Centers, Women's Business Centers, Service Corps of Retired Executives [SCORE], and Veterans Business Outreach Centers [VBOCs]). In addition, the SBA's Office of Veterans Business Development (OVBD) administers several programs to assist veteran-owned small businesses.[3]

In recent years, the SBA has focused increased attention on meeting the needs of veteran small business owners and veterans interested in starting a business, especially veterans who are transitioning from military to civilian life. For example, in FY2012, the SBA's OVBD launched the Operation Boots to Business: From Service to Startup initiative, "a comprehensive veteran entrepreneurship initiative for transitioning servicemembers."[4] More than 20,000 servicemembers

---

[1] For further information and analysis concerning the Small Business Administration's (SBA's) entrepreneurial education programs, see CRS Report R41352, *Small Business Management and Technical Assistance Training Programs*, by Robert Jay Dilger. For further information and analysis concerning the SBA's access to capital programs, see CRS Report R41146, *Small Business Administration 7(a) Loan Guaranty Program*, by Robert Jay Dilger and CRS Report R41184, *Small Business Administration 504/CDC Loan Guaranty Program*, by Robert Jay Dilger. For further information and analysis of the SBA's federal contracting programs, see CRS Report R42981, *Set-Asides for Small Businesses: Legal Requirements and Issues*, by Kate M. Manuel and Erika K. Lunder; and CRS Report R42390, *Federal Contracting and Subcontracting with Small Businesses: Issues in the 112th Congress*, by Kate M. Manuel and Erika K. Lunder.

[2] SBA, "Disaster Assistance Program: SOP 50-30-7," May 13, 2011, p. 48, at http://www.sba.gov/sites/default/files/SOP%2050%2030%207.pdf; and 13 C.F.R. §123.508. For further information and analysis concerning the SBA's disaster assistance loan program, see CRS Report R41309, *The SBA Disaster Loan Program: Overview and Possible Issues for Congress*, by Bruce R. Lindsay.

[3] SBA, "FY2015 Congressional Budget Justification and FY2013 Annual Performance Report," p. 81, at http://www.sba.gov/sites/default/files/files/FY%202015%20CBJ%20FY%202013%20APR%20FINAL%20508(1).pdf.

[4] SBA, "FY2013 Congressional Budget Justification and FY2011 Annual Performance Report," p. 62, at http://www.sba.gov/sites/default/files/files/FY%202013%20CBJ%20FY%202011%20APR.pdf; and SBA, "Operation Boots to Business: From Service to Startup," at http://www.sba.gov/bootstobusiness.

participated in the Boots to Business program in FY2012.[5] The Obama Administration requested, and Congress approved, $7 million to expand the Boots to Business program in FY2014.[6] The additional funds will enable the SBA to expand the program "nationwide to the 250,000 yearly transitioning servicemembers in all branches of the military."[7] The SBA has also announced that the program "will become a standard portion of the curricula offered at the revised Transition Assistance Program (TAP) to servicemembers," which is administered by the Department of Defense (DOD) in cooperation with the Department of Labor (DOL), Department of Veterans Affairs (VA), Department of Education (DOE), Department of Homeland Security (DHS), Office of Personnel Management (OPM), and the SBA.[8]

Congressional interest in the SBA's veteran assistance programs has increased in recent years primarily due to reports by veteran organizations that veterans were experiencing difficulty accessing the SBA's programs. Congress also has a continuing interest in assisting veterans, especially those returning from overseas in recent years, transition from military to civilian life. Although the unemployment rate (as of September 2014) among veterans (4.7%) was lower than for nonveterans 18 years and older (5.7%), the unemployment rate of veterans who have left the military since September 2001 (6.2%) was higher than the unemployment rate for nonveterans.[9]

The expansion of federal employment training programs targeted at specific populations, such as women and veterans, has also led some Members and organizations to ask if these programs should be consolidated. In their view, eliminating program duplication among federal business assistance programs across federal agencies, and within the SBA, would result in lower costs and improved services. Others argue that keeping these business assistance programs separate enables them to offer services that match the unique needs of various underserved populations, such as veterans. In their view, instead of considering program consolidation as a policy option, the focus should be on improving communication and cooperation among the federal agencies providing assistance to entrepreneurs.

---

[5] SBA, "FY2014 Congressional Budget Justification and FY2012 Annual Performance Report," p. 65, at http://www.sba.gov/sites/default/files/files/1-FY%202014%20CBJ%20FY%202012%20APR.PDF.

[6] Ibid., p. 52. Recommended funding levels for the SBA's non-credit programs are provided in the Explanatory Statement accompanying the Consolidated Appropriations Act, 2014 (Division E- Financial Services and General Government Appropriations Act, 2014), pp. 37-39, available at http://docs house.gov/billsthisweek/20140113/113-HR3547-JSOM-D-F.pdf.

[7] SBA, "FY2014 Congressional Budget Justification and FY2012 Annual Performance Report," p. 52, at http://www.sba.gov/sites/default/files/files/1-FY%202014%20CBJ%20FY%202012%20APR.PDF.

[8] The Department of Defense introduced a redesigned curriculum for the TAP program, called the Transition Goals Plans Success pilot program (Transition GPS), at seven military bases in the summer of 2012. Transition GPS is now offered nationwide. It includes a five-day core program intended to ensure that servicemembers are "career ready" when they leave military service. The core curriculum includes the following modules: pre-separation counseling (4 hours), Department of Veterans Affairs benefits (6 hours), employment workshop (24 hours), financial planning (4 hours), resilient transition (1 hour), and a crosswalk between military and civilian skills that includes a "skills gap" analysis (2 hours). Transition GPS is mandatory for nearly all exiting servicemembers. See U.S. Department of Defense, "Turbo Tap," at http://www.turbotap.org/register.tpp; and CRS Report R42790, *Employment for Veterans: Trends and Programs*, coordinated by Benjamin Collins.

[9] U.S. Department of Labor (DOL), Bureau of Labor Statistics, "Table A-5. Employment status of the civilian population 18 years and older by veteran status, period of service, and sex, not seasonally adjusted," at http://www.bls.gov/news.release/empsit.t05 htm. Media reports typically cite national employment and unemployment statistics for adults aged 16 and older. Discussions of the employment and unemployment experiences of veterans usually use the employment and unemployment experiences of adults aged 18 years and older.

This report examines the current economic circumstances of veteran-owned businesses drawn from the Bureau of the Census's 2007 Survey of Business Owners, which was administered in 2008 and 2009 and released on May 17, 2011.[10] It provides a brief overview of veterans' employment experiences, comparing unemployment and labor force participation rates for veterans, veterans who have left the military since September 2001, and nonveterans.[11] The report also describes the employment assistance programs offered by several federal agencies to assist veterans transitioning from the military to the civilian labor force and examines, in greater detail, the SBA's veteran business development programs, the SBA's efforts to enhance veterans' access to capital, and the SBA's veteran contracting programs. It also discusses the SBA's Military Reservist Economic Injury Disaster Loan program.

An Economic Profile of Veteran-Owned Businesses

Every five years since 1972, for years ending in "2" and "7," the U.S. Bureau of the Census has sent a questionnaire to a stratified random sample of nonfarm businesses in the United States that file Internal Revenue Service tax forms as individual proprietorships, partnerships, or any type of corporation, and with receipts of $1,000 or more.[12] The questionnaire asks for information about the characteristics of the businesses and their owners. Approximately 2.3 million businesses received the 2007 Survey of Business Owners (SBO), and about 62% of these businesses responded to the survey.[13] The SBO provides "the only comprehensive, regularly collected source of information on selected economic and demographic characteristics for businesses and business owners by gender, ethnicity, race, and veteran status."[14]

The Census Bureau uses information from the SBO to provide estimates of the number of employer and nonemployer firms and their sales and receipts, annual payroll, and employment. Data aggregates are provided by gender, ethnicity, race, and veteran status for the United States by 2007 North American Industry Classification System (NAICS) classification; by the kind of business; and by state, metropolitan and micropolitan statistical area, and county. The information obtained from the SBO was combined with data collected through the Census Bureau's main economic census and administrative records to provide a variety of searchable data products on Census's website, http://www.census.gov/econ/sbo/, including the most detailed economic information available on veterans and veteran-owned firms.

---

[10] U.S. Bureau of the Census, "Survey of Business Owners," at http://www.census.gov/econ/sbo/index.html.

[11] The Bureau of the Census 2012 Survey of Business Owners (SBO) is currently under way. Data from the 2012 SBO concerning veteran-owned businesses are expected to be released in November 2015. See U.S. Bureau of the Census, "2012 Survey of Business Owners Tentative Release Schedule," at http://www.census.gov/econ/sbo/releaseschedule12.html.

[12] U.S. Bureau of the Census, "Survey of Business Owners: About the Survey," at http://www.census.gov/econ/sbo/about.html.

[13] U.S. Bureau of the Census, "Survey of Business Owners: 2007 Methodology," at http://www.census.gov/econ/sbo/methodology.html.

[14] U.S. Bureau of the Census, "Survey of Business Owners," at http://www.census.gov/econ/sbo/about.html.

Demographics

The Bureau of the Census estimates that in 2007 about 9.0% of nonfarm firms in the United States (2,447,608 of 27,092,908) were owned by veterans.[15] Four states had more than 100,000 veteran-owned firms: California (239,422), Texas (199,476), New York (127,156), and Florida (176,727). Of the nearly 2.45 million veteran-owned firms in 2007,

- 79.9% (1,956,259) had no paid employees and 20.1% (491,349) had paid employees. This ratio is very similar to comparable national figures for 2007, according to which 78.8% of nonfarm firms had no paid employees (21,357,346) and 21.2% had paid employees (5,735,562).[16]

- 99.8% (490,560) had fewer than 500 employees and 0.2% (789) had at least 500 employees. This ratio is very similar to comparable national figures for 2007, according to which 99.7% (5,717,830) had fewer than 500 employees and 0.3% (17,732) had at least 500 employees.[17]

- 94.8% (2,320,291) were owned by a male, 4.0% were owned by a female (97,114), and 1.2% (29,593) were owned equally by a male and a female. Veteran-owned firms were more likely than other firms in 2007 to be owned by a male. The comparable national figures for 2007 are 52.9% (13,900,554) of nonfarm firms were owned by a male, 29.6% were owned by a female (7,792,115), and 17.5% (4,602,192) were owned equally by a male and a female.[18]

- 90.7% (2,219,385) were owned by a Caucasian, 7.7% (188,820) were owned by an African American, 1.3% (32,732) were owned by an Asian, 1.1% (27,111) were owned by an American Indian or Alaska Indian, 0.2% (4,123) were owned by a native Hawaiian or other Pacific Islander, and 0.1% (3,096) were owned by "some other race." Veteran-owned firms were somewhat more likely than other firms in 2007 to be owned by a Caucasian and somewhat less likely to be owned by an Asian. The comparable national figures for 2007 are 83.4% (22,595,146)

---

[15] An additional 1.2 million nonfarm U.S. firms (about 4.5% of all nonfarm U.S. firms) were owned equally (50%-50%) by veterans and nonveterans. See U.S. Bureau of the Census, "Statistics for All U.S. Firms by Industry, Veteran Status, and Receipts Size of Firm for the U.S. and States: 2007," at http://factfinder2.census.gov/faces/tableservices/jsf/pages/productview xhtml?pid=SBO_2007_00CSA08&prodType=table. Veteran status was based on self-identification. Respondents were asked to report if a business owner is a veteran of the U.S. military service including the Coast Guard. Businesses could be categorized as: veteran-owned (U.S. military service veterans own 51% or more of the equity, interest, or stock of the business); equally veteran/nonveteran-owned (50% veteran and 50% nonveteran ownership of the equity, interest, or stock of the business); or nonveteran-owned (nonveterans own 51% or more of the equity, interest, or stock of the business).

[16] U.S. Bureau of the Census, "American Fact Finder: Statistics for All U.S. Firms by Industry, Veteran Status, and Race for the U.S., States, Metro Areas, Counties, and Places: 2007," at http://factfinder2.census.gov/faces/tableservices/jsf/pages/productview.xhtml?pid=SBO_2007_00CSA04&prodType=table.

[17] Of veteran-owned firms, 90.3% (443,495) had fewer than 20 employees, 8.2% (40,406) had 20 employees to 99 employees, and 1.4% (6,659) had 100 employees to 499 employees. See U.S. Bureau of the Census, "American Fact Finder: Statistics for All U.S. Firms With Paid Employees by Industry, Veteran Status, and Employment Size of Firm for the U.S. and States: 2007," at http://factfinder2.census.gov/faces/tableservices/jsf/pages/productview xhtml?pid=SBO_2007_00CSA12&prodType=table.

[18] U.S. Bureau of the Census, "American Fact Finder: Statistics for All U.S. Firms by Industry, Veteran Status, and Gender for the U.S., States, Metro Areas, Counties, and Places: 2007," at http://factfinder2.census.gov/faces/tableservices/jsf/pages/productview.xhtml?pid=SBO_2007_00CSA02&prodType=table.

---

were owned by a Caucasian, 7.1% (1,921,864) were owned by an African American, 5.7% (1,549,559) were owned by an Asian, 0.9% (236,691) were owned by an American Indian or Alaska Indian, 0.1% (37,687) were owned by a native Hawaiian or other Pacific Islander, and 0.3% (80,777) were owned by "some other race."[19]

- 2.8% (68,891) were owned by an individual under the age of 35, 22.1% (543,359) were owned by an individual aged 35 years to 54 years, and 75.1% (1,841,809) were owned by an individual aged 55 years or older. Veteran-owned firms were more likely than other firms in 2007 to be owned by an individual aged 55 years or older. The comparable national figures for 2007 are 12.6% (2,535,187) of nonfarm firms were owned by an individual under the age of 35; 50.8% (10,196,376) were owned by an individual aged 35 years to 54 years; and 36.5% (7,332,182) were owned by an individual aged 55 years or older.[20]

- 8.3% (196,760) were owned by an individual who reported that he or she had a service-connected disability.[21]

Employment, Payroll, and Receipts

In 2007, veteran-owned employer firms

- employed 5.8 million persons (about 4.9% of total U.S. employment);

- reported a total payroll of $210.0 billion (about 4.4% of total U.S. payroll);

- generated $1.125 trillion in total receipts (about 4.1% of total U.S. receipts); and

- had average receipts of $2.3 million.[22]

In 2007, veteran-owned nonemployer firms

- generated 7.7% ($93.8 billion) of the total receipts generated by veteran-owned firms; and

- had average receipts of $47,931.

The comparable national figures for receipts in 2007 were $45,544 for all nonemployer firms and $5.1 million for all employer firms.[23]

---

[19] The total percentage exceeds 100 because each owner had the option of selecting more than one race and was included in each race selected. See U.S. Bureau of the Census, "American Fact Finder: Statistics for All U.S. Firms by Industry, Veteran Status, and Race for the U.S., States, Metro Areas, Counties, and Places: 2007," at http://factfinder2.census.gov/faces/tableservices/jsf/pages/productview xhtml?pid=SBO_2007_00CSA04&prodType=table.

[20] U.S. Bureau of the Census, "American Fact Finder: Statistics for Owners of Respondent Firms by Owner's Age by Gender, Ethnicity, Race, and Veteran Status for the U.S.: 2007," at http://factfinder2.census.gov/faces/tableservices/jsf/pages/productview xhtml?pid=SBO_2007_00CSCBO08&prodType=table.

[21] U.S. Bureau of the Census, "American Fact Finder: Statistics for Veteran Owners of Respondent Firms by Owner's Service-Disabled Veteran Status and Gender for the U.S.: 2007," at http://factfinder2.census.gov/faces/tableservices/jsf/pages/productview.xhtml?pid=SBO_2007_00CSCBO10&prodType=table.

[22] U.S. Bureau of the Census, "American Fact Finder: Statistics for All U.S. Firms With Paid Employees by Veteran Status and Number of States in Which They Operate: 2007," at http://factfinder2.census.gov/faces/tableservices/jsf/pages/productview xhtml?pid=SBO_2007_00CSA20&prodType=table.

Access to Capital

As shown in **Table 1**, the source of capital most frequently used by veterans to start or acquire a business in 2007 was personal or family savings (811,388 veterans, or 61.7% of respondents), followed by a business loan from a bank or financial institution (128,895 veterans, or 9.8% of respondents), a personal or business credit card (114,012 veterans, or 8.7% of respondents), and personal or family assets other than the owner's savings (98,113 veterans, or 7.5% of respondents).

**Table 1. Source of Capital for Veteran Business Owners
Starting or Acquiring Their Businesses, 2007**

Source of Capital	Number of Veteran Respondents	% of Veteran Respondents
Personal or Family Savings	811,388	61.7%
Business Loan from a Bank or Financial Institution	128,895	9.8%
Personal or Business Credit Card	114,012	8.7%
Personal or Family Assets Other Than the Owner's Savings	98,113	7.5%
Personal or Family Home Equity Loan	55,736	4.2%
Business Loan or Investment from Family or Friends	25,038	1.9%
Government-Guaranteed Business Loan from a Bank or Financial Institution	8,305	0.6%
Business Loan from a Federal, State, or Local Government	8,001	0.6%
Investment from Venture Capitalists	3,664	0.3%
Grant	1,364	0.1%
Other Source(s) of Capital	23,825	1.8%
Did Not Need Any Capital to Start or Acquire Their Business	284,505	21.6%
Did Not Recall Where They Received the Capital to Start or Acquire Their Business	40,390	3.1%

Source: U.S. Bureau of the Census, "American Fact Finder: Statistics for All U.S. Firms by Sources of Capital Used to Start or Acquire the Business by Industry, Gender, Ethnicity, Race, and Veteran Status for the U.S.: 2007," at http://factfinder2.census.gov/faces/tableservices/jsf/pages/productview.xhtml?pid= SBO_2007_00CSCB13&prodType=table.

Note: The total percentage exceeds 100 because each owner had the option of selecting more than one source of capital.

(...continued)

[23] Ibid.

As shown in **Table 2**, the source of capital most frequently used by veterans to expand or make capital improvements to an existing business in 2007 was personal or family savings (384,517 veterans, or 30.0% of respondents). The next most frequently used source of capital to expand or make capital improvements to an existing business was a personal or business credit card (139,260 veterans, or 10.9% of respondents), followed by business profits or assets (138,440 veterans, or 10.8% of respondents), and a business loan from a bank or financial institution (107,614 veterans, or 8.4% of respondents).

Table 2. Source of Capital for Veteran Businesses Owners Expanding or Making Capital Improvements to Their Businesses, 2007

Source of Capital	Number of Veteran Respondents	% of Veteran Respondents
Personal or Family Savings	384,517	30.0%
Personal or Business Credit Card	139,260	10.9%
Business Profits or Assets	138,440	10.8%
Business Loan from a Bank or Financial Institution	107,614	8.4%
Personal or Family Assets Other Than the Owner's Savings	54,479	4.3%
Personal or Family Home Equity Loan	50,793	4.0%
Business Loan or Investment from Family or Friends	9,720	0.8%
Business Loan from a Federal, State, or Local Government	4,938	0.4%
Government-Guaranteed Business Loan from a Bank or Financial Institution	4,511	0.4%
Investment from Venture Capitalists	1,591	0.1%
Grant	1,438	0.1%
Other Source(s) of Capital	9,200	0.7%
Did Not Expand or Make Capital Improvements In 2007	631,242	49.3%
Did Not Recall Where They Received the Capital to Expand or Make Capital Improvements to Their Business	18,692	3.7%

Source: U.S. Bureau of the Census, "American Fact Finder: Statistics for All U.S. Firms by Sources Used to Finance Expansion or Capital Improvements by Industry, Gender, Ethnicity, Race, and Veteran Status for the U.S.: 2007," at http://factfinder2.census.gov/faces/tableservices/jsf/pages/productview.xhtml?pid= SBO_2007_00CSCB28&prodType=table.

Note: The total percentage exceeds 100 because each owner had the option of selecting more than one source of capital.

Veterans' Employment Data

The Department of Labor's Bureau of Labor Statistics (BLS) provides monthly updates of the employment status of the nation's veterans. The BLS reports that as of September 2014, there were 21.1 million veterans.[24] There were 10.8 million veterans in the civilian labor force (i.e., they were either employed or unemployed and available for work, except for temporary illness, and had made specific efforts to find employment sometime during the four-week period ending with the reference week). Of those veterans in the civilian labor force, about 10.3 million were employed and about 511,000 were unemployed.[25]

As of September 2014, veterans, as a group, had a lower unemployment rate (4.7%) than nonveterans aged 18 years and older (5.7%), and veterans also had a lower labor force participation rate (the percentage of the available workforce that is employed or actively seeking employment) than nonveterans aged 18 years and older (51.4% compared with 65.6%).[26] A report by the Council of Economic Advisers and the National Economic Council attributed the lower labor force participation rate for veterans to several factors, including the difficulty many civilian employers have in understanding a military resume and how military job titles translate into civilian job skills, the presence of a service-connected disability, especially among the post-9/11 veteran population, and the number of post-9/11 veterans (about 217,000) who have been diagnosed with post-traumatic stress disorder.[27]

The employment experiences of veterans who left the military since September 2001 differ somewhat from the employment experiences of veterans who left the military before September 2001. As of September 2014, veterans who left the military since September 2001 had both higher levels of unemployment (6.2% compared with 4.3%) and higher levels of labor force participation (78.4% compared with 46.4%) than veterans who left the military before September 2001. The higher labor force participation rate for veterans who left the military since September 2001 was not wholly unexpected. They entered the civilian workforce more recently and have had less time to develop a reason (e.g., health issue, family responsibility, discouragement, retirement) to withdraw from the civilian workforce than veterans who left the military before September 2001.

Veterans' Employment and Business Development Programs

Several federal agencies, including the SBA, sponsor employment and business development programs to assist veterans in their transition from the military into the civilian labor force. As will be discussed, the expansion of federal employment and business development training programs targeted at specific populations, such as women and veterans, has led some Members

---

[24] DOL, Bureau of Labor Statistics, "Table A-5. Employment status of the civilian population 18 years and over by veteran status, period of service, and sex, not seasonally adjusted," at http://www.bls.gov/news release/empsit.t05.htm.

[25] Ibid.

[26] Ibid.

[27] Executive Office of the President, Council of Economic Advisers and the National Economic Council, "Military Skills for America's Future: Leveraging Military Service and Experience to Put Veterans and Military Spouses Back to Work," May 31, 2012, pp. 4-6, at http://www.whitehouse.gov/sites/default/files/docs/veterans_report_5-31-2012.pdf. The report indicated that military spouses also face a number of employment barriers. For example, military spouses are "ten times more likely to have moved across state lines in the last year compared to their civilian counterparts," affecting job tenure, advancement opportunities, and, for those in occupations requiring a state-specific occupational license or certification, the need to re-qualify for their license or certification after moving across state lines. See ibid., pp. 8-10.

and organizations to ask if these programs should be consolidated. Others question if the level of communication and coordination among federal agencies administering these programs has been sufficient to ensure the programs are being administered in the most efficient and effective manner.

The SBA's Veterans Business Development Programs

In an effort to assist veteran entrepreneurs, the SBA has either provided or supported management and technical assistance training for veteran-owned small businesses since its formation as an agency.[28] In FY2013, the SBA provided management and technical assistance training services to more than 100,000 veterans through its various management and technical assistance training partners (e.g., Small Business Development Centers, Women's Business Centers, Service Corps of Retired Executives [SCORE], and Veterans Business Outreach Centers [VBOCs]).[29] In addition, the SBA's OVBD administers several programs to assist veteran-owned businesses, including

- the Entrepreneurship Bootcamp for Veterans with Disabilities Consortium of Universities, which provides "experiential training in entrepreneurship and small business management to post-9/11 veterans with disabilities" at eight universities;[30]

- the Veteran Women Igniting the Spirit of Entrepreneurship (V-WISE) program, administered through a cooperative agreement with Syracuse University, which offers women veterans a 15-day, online course focused on entrepreneurship skills and the "language of business," followed by a 3-day conference (offered twice a year at varying locations) in which participants "are exposed to successful entrepreneurs and CEOs of Fortune 500 companies and leaders in government" and participate in courses on business planning, marketing, accounting and finance, operations and production, human resources, and work-life balance;[31]

- the Operation Endure and Grow Program, administered through a cooperative agreement with Syracuse University, which offers an eight-week online training program "focused on the fundamentals of launching and/or growing a small business" and is available to National Guard and reservists and their family members;[32]

- the Boots to Business program, administered in partnership with DOD, which provides "an entrepreneurship training component as part of the re-design of the military's Transition Assistance Program" composed of "three progressive

---

[28] U.S. Congress, Senate Committee on Banking and Currency, *Extension of the Small Business Act of 1953*, report to accompany S. 2127, 84th Cong., 1st sess., July 22, 1955, S.Rept. 84-1350 (Washington: GPO, 1955), p. 17.

[29] SBA, "FY2015 Congressional Budget Justification and FY2013 Annual Performance Report," p. 81, at http://www.sba.gov/sites/default/files/files/FY%202015%20CBJ%20FY%202013%20APR%20FINAL%20508(1).pdf.

[30] Syracuse University, "About the EBV," Syracuse, NY, at http://whitman.syr.edu/ebv/about/.

[31] Syracuse University, "Women Veterans Igniting the Spirit of Entrepreneurship (V-WISE)," Syracuse, NY, at http://whitman.syr.edu/vwise/about.aspx.

[32] Syracuse University, "About Operation Endure and Grow," Syracuse, NY, at http://vets.syr.edu/education/endure-grow/.

phases to deliver exposure, introduction, and opt-in comprehensive training for servicemembers interested in business ownership";[33] and

- the VBOC program, which provides veterans and their spouses management and technical assistance training at 15 locations, including assistance with the development and maintenance of a 5-year business plan and referrals to other SBA resource partners when appropriate for additional training or mentoring services.[34]

The SBA indicated in its FY2015 congressional budget justification document that "in the coming years, more than a quarter of a million service members will transition from active service every year."[35] To help meet veteran entrepreneurs' needs, the SBA indicated that, in addition to expanding the Boots to Business program, in FY2015 it will "work to increase accessibility to veterans, guardsmen, and reservists who are not eligible for transition services" by, among other activities,

- expanding the Entrepreneurial Bootcamp for Veterans with Disabilities program, increasing both the number of course offerings and the number of participating business schools in the consortium;[36]

- reinstating funding for VBOCs "engaging in the Department of Defense Yellow Ribbon Reintegration Program events for Guard and reserve members returning from deployment";[37] and

- expanding the capacity of the V-WISE program to include "more cities serving more than 1,200 additional women veterans."[38]

The SBA also continues to work closely with the Interagency Task Force for Veterans Small Business Development, which was established by executive order on April 26, 2010, held its first

---

[33] SBA, "FY2015 Congressional Budget Justification and FY2013 Annual Performance Report," p. 52, at http://www.sba.gov/sites/default/files/files/ FY%202015%20CBJ%20FY%202013%20APR%20FINAL%20508%281%29.pdf. "Phase 1 includes a short video introduction on entrepreneurship with a call to action for returning veterans to consider entrepreneurship and with a description of the career path. Phase 2 includes classroom instruction with a 90 minute in person training course on entrepreneurship. Phase 3 includes online instruction via an eight-week online distance learning course that leads to the creation of a business plan." See ibid.

[34] SBA, "Veterans Business Outreach Centers," at http://www.sba.gov/content/veterans-business-outreach-centers/. Each Veterans Business Outreach Center is funded on an annual basis, with funding not to exceed $150,000 each year. Awards "may vary, depending upon location, staff size, project objectives, performance and agency priorities, and additional special initiatives initiated by the Office of Veterans Business Development." See SBA, Office of Veterans Business Development, "Special Program Announcement: Veterans Business Outreach Center Program," April 2010, p. 2, at http://archive.sba.gov/idc/groups/public/documents/sba_program_office/ovbd_vboc_prgm_announce2010.pdf. Also, existing centers may receive additional funding for special outreach or other initiatives. The initial grant award is for 12 months, with the possibility of 4 additional (option) years. In FY2013, the Veterans Business Outreach Centers Program conducted its ninth annual "Customer Satisfaction Survey." The FY2013 survey found that 91% of the clients using the centers were satisfied or highly satisfied with the quality, relevance, and timeliness of the assistance provided. See SBA, "FY2015 Congressional Budget Justification and FY2013 Annual Performance Report," p. 81, at http://www.sba.gov/sites/default/files/files/FY%202015%20CBJ%20FY%202013%20APR%20FINAL%20508(1).pdf.

[35] SBA, "FY2015 Congressional Budget Justification and FY2013 Annual Performance Report," p. 80, at http://www.sba.gov/sites/default/files/files/FY%202015%20CBJ%20FY%202013%20APR%20FINAL%20508(1).pdf.

[36] Ibid., pp. 82-83.

[37] Ibid., p. 83.

[38] Ibid.

---

public meeting on October 15, 2010, and issued its first report on November 1, 2011, to identify "gaps in ensuring that transitioning military members who are interested in owning a small business get needed assistance and training."[39] The task force's second report, issued on November 29, 2012, focused on progress made since the initial report.[40] The task force continues to meet on a quarterly basis to foster communication and monitor agency progress in assisting transitioning servicemembers.

Congressional Issues: Duplication of Services

The SBA's OVBD, which serves as the SBA's focal point for its veteran assistance programs, was created by P.L. 106-50, the Veterans Entrepreneurship and Small Business Development Act of 1999. The act addressed congressional concerns that the United States generally, and the SBA in particular, was not, at that time, doing enough to meet the needs of veteran entrepreneurs, especially service-disabled veteran entrepreneurs.[41] At that time, several Members of Congress argued that "the needs of veterans have been diminished systematically at the SBA" as evidenced by the agency's elimination of direct loans, including direct loans to veterans, in 1995; and a decline in the SBA's "training and counseling for veterans ... from 38,775 total counseling sessions for veterans in 1993 to 29,821 sessions in 1998."[42] To address these concerns, the act authorized the establishment of the federally chartered National Veterans Business Development Corporation (known as the Veterans Corporation and reconstituted, without a federal charter, in 2012 as Veteranscorp.org).[43] Its mission is to

> (1) expand the provision of and improve access to technical assistance regarding entrepreneurship for the Nation's veterans; and (2) to assist veterans, including service-disabled veterans, with the formation and expansion of small business concerns by working with and organizing public and private resources, including those of the Small Business Administration, the Department of Veterans Affairs, the Department of Labor, the Department of Commerce, the Department of Defense, the Service Corps of Retired

---

[39] SBA, Office of Veterans Business Development, "Interagency Task Force," at http://www.sba.gov/about-offices-content/1/2985/resources/14372; and The Interagency Task Force on Veterans Small Business Development, "Report to the President: Empowering Veterans Through Entrepreneurship," November 1, 2011, at http://www.sba.gov/sites/default/files/FY2012-Final%20Veterans%20TF%20Report%20to%20President.pdf.

[40] The Interagency Task Force on Veterans Small Business Development, "Heroes on the Home Front: Supporting Veteran Success as Small Business Owners," November 29, 2012, at http://www.sba.gov/sites/default/files/files/Veterans_Report_FINAL.pdf. The Interagency Task Force on Veterans Small Business Development includes senior-level representatives of the SBA, the Departments of Defense, Labor, Treasury, and Veterans Affairs, the General Services Administration, the Office of Management and Budget, and four representatives from veterans' service or military organizations appointed by the SBA administrator. SBA Associate Administrator Rhett Jeppson serves as its chair. See Executive Order 13540, "Interagency Task Force on Veterans Small Business Development," 75 *Federal Register* 22497-22498, April 29, 2010; and U.S Small Business Administration, "Inter-Agency Task Force on Veterans Small Business Development: Kick Off Meeting Wednesday, September 15, 2010," at http://www.sba.gov/about-sba-info/14368.

[41] P.L. 106-50, the Veterans Entrepreneurship and Small Business Development Act of 1999, Section 101. Findings.

[42] U.S. Congress, House Committee on Small Business, *Veterans Entrepreneurship and Small Business Development Act of 1999*, report to accompany H.R. 1568, 106th Cong., 1st sess., June 29, 1999, H.Rept. 106-206 (Washington: GPO, 1999), pp. 14-15.

[43] Veteranscorp, "About Us," Oxford, MD at http://www.veteranscorp.org/2012/01/a-new-veteranscorp-org-gets-the-chance-to-help-veteran-entrepreneurs-2/.

Executives …, the Small Business Development Centers …, and the business development staffs of each department and agency of the United States.[44]

P.L. 106-50 reemphasized the SBA's responsibility "to reach out to and include veterans in its programs providing financial and technical assistance."[45] It included veterans as a target group for the SBA's 7(a), 504 Certified Development Company (504/CDC), and Microloan lending programs. It also required the SBA to enter into a memorandum of understanding with SCORE to, among other things, establish "a program to coordinate counseling and training regarding entrepreneurship to veterans through the chapters of SCORE throughout the United States."[46] In addition, it directed the SBA to enter into a memorandum of understanding with small business development centers, the VA, and the National Veterans Business Development Corporation "with respect to entrepreneurial assistance to veterans, including service-disabled veterans."[47] The act specified that the following services were to be provided:

(1) Conducting of studies and research, and the distribution of information generated by such studies and research, on the formation, management, financing, marketing, and operation of small business concerns by veterans.

(2) Provision of training and counseling to veterans concerning the formation, management, financing, marketing, and operation of small business concerns.

(3) Provision of management and technical assistance to the owners and operators of small business concerns regarding international markets, the promotion of exports, and the transfer of technology.

(4) Provision of assistance and information to veterans regarding procurement opportunities with Federal, State, and local agencies, especially such agencies funded in whole or in part with Federal funds.

(5) Establishment of an information clearinghouse to collect and distribute information, including by electronic means, on the assistance programs of Federal, State, and local governments, and of the private sector, including information on office locations, key personnel, telephone numbers, mail and electronic addresses, and contracting and subcontracting opportunities.

(6) Provision of Internet or other distance learning academic instruction for veterans in business subjects, including accounting, marketing, and business fundamentals.

(7) Compilation of a list of small business concerns owned and controlled by service-disabled veterans that provide products or services that could be procured by the United States and delivery of such list to each department and agency of the United States. Such list

---

[44] P.L. 106-50, the Veterans Entrepreneurship and Small Business Development Act of 1999, Section 33. National Veterans Business Development Corporation. Also, see 15 U.S.C. §657c.

[45] U.S. Congress, House Committee on Small Business, *Veterans Entrepreneurship and Small Business Development Act of 1999*, report to accompany H.R. 1568, 106th Cong., 1st sess., June 29, 1999, H.Rept. 106-206 (Washington: GPO, 1999), p. 14.

[46] P.L. 106-50, the Veterans Entrepreneurship and Small Business Development Act of 1999, Section 301. Score Program.

[47] Ibid., Section 302. Entrepreneurial Assistance.

shall be delivered in hard copy and electronic form and shall include the name and address of each such small business concern and the products or services that it provides.[48]

The SBA's OVBD was established to address these statutory requirements by promoting "veterans' small business ownership by conducting comprehensive outreach, through program and policy development and implementation, ombudsman support, coordinated agency initiatives, and direct assistance to veterans, service-disabled veterans, reserve and National Guard members, and discharging active duty servicemembers and their families."[49]

As mentioned previously, the OVBD provided, or supported third parties in providing, management and technical assistance training services to more than 100,000 veterans during FY2013.[50] These services were provided

> through funded SBA district office outreach; OVBD-developed and distributed materials; websites; partnering with DOD [Department of Defense], DOL [Department of Labor] and universities; agreements with regional veterans business outreach centers; direct guidance, training and assistance to Agency veteran customers; and through enhancements to intra-agency programs used by the military and veteran communities.[51]

The expansion of the SBA's outreach efforts to veterans has led some Members and organizations to ask if the nation's veterans might be better served if some of the veteran employment and business development programs offered by federal agencies were consolidated. For example, as mentioned previously, DOD, in cooperation with several federal agencies, operates the recently revised Transition Assistance Program, Transition GPS, which provides employment information and training to exiting servicemembers to assist them in transitioning from the military into the civilian labor force. In addition, DOL's Jobs for Veterans State Grants program provides states funding for Disabled Veterans' Outreach Program specialists and Local Veterans' Employment Representatives to provide outreach and assistance to veterans, and their spouses, seeking employment.[52] DOL also administers the Veterans Workforce Investment Program, which provides grants to fund programs operated by eligible state and local government workforce investment boards, state and local government agencies, and private nonprofit organizations to provide various services designed to assist veterans' transitions into the civilian labor force.[53] The DOL-administered Homeless Veterans Reintegration Program provides grants to fund programs operated by eligible state and local government workforce investment boards, state and local government agencies, and private nonprofit organizations that provide various services designed

---

[48] Ibid.

[49] SBA, "FY2013 Congressional Budget Justification and FY2011 Annual Performance Report," p. 62, at http://www.sba.gov/sites/default/files/files/FY%202013%20CBJ%20FY%202011%20APR.pdf.

[50] SBA, "FY2015 Congressional Budget Justification and FY2013 Annual Performance Report," p. 81, at http://www.sba.gov/sites/default/files/files/FY%202015%20CBJ%20FY%202013%20APR%20FINAL%20508(1).pdf.

[51] SBA, "FY2013 Congressional Budget Justification and FY2011 Annual Performance Report," p. 62, at http://www.sba.gov/sites/default/files/files/FY%202013%20CBJ%20FY%202011%20APR.pdf.

[52] For information on the Disabled Veterans' Outreach Program and Local Veterans' Employment Representatives Program see DOL, "Jobs for Veterans State Grants," at http://www.dol.gov/vets/grants/state/jvsg htm.

[53] For further information and analysis of federal programs outside of the SBA that are designed to assist veterans seeking civilian employment, see CRS Report RS22666, *Veterans Benefits: Federal Employment Assistance*, by Christine Scott.

to assist homeless veterans achieve meaningful employment and to aid in the development of a service delivery system to address problems facing homeless veterans.[54]

Advocates of consolidating veteran employment and business development programs argue that eliminating program duplication among federal agencies would result in lower costs and improved services. For example, H.R. 4072, the Consolidating Veteran Employment Services for Improved Performance Act of 2012, which was introduced during the 112th Congress and ordered to be reported by the House Committee on Veterans' Affairs on April 27, 2012, would have transferred several veteran employment training programs from the DOL to the VA.[55]

Also, in 2011, 2012, 2013, and 2014, the House Committee on Small Business, in its "Views and Estimates" letter to the House Committee on the Budget, recommended that funding for the SBA's VBOCs be eliminated (saving approximately $2.5 million) because, as it stated in 2012, "the SBA already provides significant assistance to veterans who are seeking to start or already operate small businesses. The VBOCs duplicate services already available from the SBA, other entrepreneurial development partners and programs available from the Department of Veterans Affairs."[56] In 2014, the House Committee on Small Business also recommended that if additional funds were to be provided to VBOCs, those funds should come from the SBA's Boots to Business initiative.

Advocates of consolidating federal veteran employment and business development programs point to various U.S. Government Accountability Office (GAO) reports that have generally characterized the broader category of federal support for entrepreneurs, including veteran entrepreneurs, as fragmented and having overlapping missions. For example, in 2012, GAO identified 53 programs within the SBA and the Departments of Commerce, Housing and Urban Development, and Agriculture designed to support entrepreneurs, including 36 programs that provide entrepreneurs technical assistance, such as business training, counseling, and research and development support. GAO found that "the overlap among these programs raise[s] questions about whether a fragmented system is the most effective way to support entrepreneurs" and suggested agencies should "determine whether there are more efficient ways to continue to serve the unique needs of entrepreneurs, including consolidating programs."[57]

---

[54] For further information and analysis concerning the Homeless Veterans Reintegration Program, see CRS Report RL34024, *Veterans and Homelessness*, by Libby Perl.

[55] U.S. House of Representatives, Committee on Veterans' Affairs, "Debunking the Myths: H.R. 4072," at http://veterans house.gov/4072.

[56] U.S. House of Representatives, Committee on Small Business, "Views and Estimates of the Committee on Small Business on Matters to be set forth in the Concurrent Resolution on the Budget for Fiscal Year 2012," March 17, 2011, at http://smallbusiness.house.gov/uploadedfiles/march_17_views_and_estimates_letter.pdf. Also, see U.S. House of Representatives, Committee on Small Business, "Views and Estimates of the Committee on Small Business on Matters to be set forth in the Concurrent Resolution on the Budget for Fiscal Year 2013," March 7, 2012, at http://smallbusiness house.gov/uploadedfiles/views_and_estimates_fy_2013.pdf; U.S. House of Representatives, Committee on Small Business, "Views and Estimates of the Committee on Small Business on Matters to be set forth in the Concurrent Resolution on the Budget for Fiscal Year 2014," February 27, 2013, at http://smallbusiness house.gov/uploadedfiles/revised_2014_views_and_estimates_document.pdf; and U.S. House of Representatives, Committee on Small Business, "Views and Estimates of the Committee on Small Business on Matters to be set forth in the Concurrent Resolution on the Budget for Fiscal Year 2015," March 25, 2014, at http://smallbusiness house.gov/uploadedfiles/3-25-2014_revised_budget_views_and_estimates__fy_2015_v2.pdf.

[57] U.S. Government Accountability Office (GAO), *2012 Annual Report: Opportunities to Reduce Duplication, Overlap and Fragmentation, Achieve Savings, and Enhance Revenue*, GAO-12-342SP, February 28, 2012, p. 55, at http://www.gao.gov/assets/590/588818.pdf. Also see GAO, *Entrepreneurial Assistance: Opportunities Exist to Improve* (continued...)

Instead of consolidating programs, some argue that improved communication and cooperation among the federal agencies providing entrepreneur support programs, and among the SBA's management and technical assistance training resource partners, would enhance program efficiencies while preserving the ability of these programs to offer services that match the unique needs of various underserved populations, such as veterans. For example, during the 111th Congress, the House passed H.R. 2352, the Job Creation Through Entrepreneurship Act of 2009, on May 20, 2009, by a vote of 406-15. The Senate did not take action on the bill. In its committee report accompanying the bill, the House Committee on Small Business concluded at that time that

> each ED [Entrepreneurial Development] program has a unique mandate and service delivery approach that is customized to its particular clients. However, as a network, the programs have established local connections and resources that benefit entrepreneurs within a region. Enhanced coordination among this network is critical to make the most of scarce resources available for small firms. It can also ensure that best practices are shared amongst providers that have similar goals but work within different contexts.[58]

The bill was designed to enhance oversight and coordination of the SBA's management and technical assistance training programs by requiring the SBA to coordinate these programs "with State and local economic development agencies and other federal agencies as appropriate" and to "report annually to Congress, in consultation with other federal departments and agencies as appropriate, on opportunities to foster coordination, limit duplication, and improve program delivery for federal entrepreneurial development activities."[59]

In a related development, as mentioned previously, the Obama Administration formed the Interagency Task Force for Veterans Small Business Development by executive order on April 26, 2010. The SBA's representative (SBA Associate Director Rhett Jeppson) chairs the task force, which is composed of senior representatives from seven federal agencies and four representatives from veterans' organizations.[60] One of the task force's goals is to improve "collaboration, integration and focus across federal agencies, key programs (e.g., the Transition Assistance Program), veterans' service organizations, states, and academia."[61]

On November 1, 2011, the task force issued its first set of recommendations, which included several recommendations designed to increase and augment federal entrepreneurial training and technical assistance programs offered to veterans. For example, it recommended the development of a "standardized, national entrepreneurship training program specifically for veterans" that "could utilize expert local instructors, including academics and successful small business owners, to provide training in skills used to create and grow entrepreneurial ventures and small business.

(...continued)

Programs' Collaboration, Data-Tracking, and Performance Management, GAO-12-819, August 23, 2012, pp. 60-61, at http://www.gao.gov/assets/650/647267.pdf.

[58] U.S. Congress, House Committee on Small Business, *Job Creation Through Entrepreneurship Act of 2009*, report to accompany H.R. 2352, 111th Cong., 1st sess., May 15, 2009, H.Rept. 111-112 (Washington: GPO, 2009), pp. 17-18.

[59] H.R. 2352, the Job Creation Through Entrepreneurship Act of 2009, Section 601. Expanding Entrepreneurship.

[60] The seven federal agencies are the SBA, U.S. General Services Administration, U.S. Office of Management and Budget, and the Departments of Defense, Labor, Treasury, and Veterans Affairs. The four veterans' organizations are Association of State Directors of Veterans Affairs, Student Veterans of America, the American Legion, and VET-Force. SBA Deputy Administrator Marie Johns served as the task force's chair until she left the agency in May 2013.

[61] Interagency Task Force on Veterans Small Business Development, "Report to the President: Empowering Veterans Through Entrepreneurship," November 1, 2011, p. 6, at http://www.sba.gov/sites/default/files/FY2012-Final%20Veterans%20TF%20Report%20to%20President.pdf.

The national program could provide engaging training modules and workshops dedicated to the basics of launching a business."[62] The task force also recommended the development of a web portal "that allows veterans to access entrepreneurship resources from across the government."[63]

The task force issued its second report on November 29, 2012. The document was essentially a progress report concerning the task force's activities since the initial report's release:

> In FY2012, the Task Force, along with the interagency Veterans Employment Initiative, developed and piloted a re-designed military transition program, entitled Transition GPS, that includes an entrepreneurship training program called "Operation Boots to Business: from Service to Startup." This program is expected to be rolled out nationally in the coming year. The Task Force has also worked to streamline programs and cut paperwork for veteran small businesses through support for initiatives such as BusinessUSA [an online website with links to over 1,000 federal and state resources, over 130 success stories, and over 3,750 events nationwide] and QuickApp for [SBA-guaranteed] surety bonds [under $250,000 featuring a streamlined application process] and it has continued the efforts begun last year to make the process of winning Federal government contracts simpler and easier for service-disabled veterans and veteran-owned small business.[64]

Veterans' Access to Capital

The SBA administers several loan guaranty programs, including the 7(a) and the 504/CDC programs, to encourage lenders to provide loans to small businesses "that might not otherwise obtain financing on reasonable terms and conditions."[65]

The SBA's 7(a) loan guaranty program is considered the agency's flagship loan guaranty program. Its name is derived from Section 7(a) of the Small Business Act of 1953 (P.L. 83-163, as amended), which authorizes the SBA to provide business loans to American small businesses.

The 7(a) loan guaranty program provides SBA-approved lenders a guaranty of up to 85% of loans of $150,000 or less and up to 75% of loans exceeding $150,000, up to the program's maximum gross loan amount of $5 million (up to $3.75 million maximum guaranty). In FY2014, the average approved 7(a) loan amount was $368,737.[66]

Proceeds from 7(a) loans may be used to establish a new business or to assist in the operation, acquisition, or expansion of an existing business. Specific uses include to acquire land (by purchase or lease); improve a site (e.g., grading, streets, parking lots, and landscaping); purchase, convert, expand, or renovate one or more existing buildings; construct one or more new

---

[62] Ibid., p. 15.

[63] Ibid., p. 8.

[64] The Interagency Task Force on Veterans Small Business Development, "Heroes on the Home Front: Supporting Veteran Success as Small Business Owners," cover letter and introductory material, November 29, 2012, at http://www.sba.gov/sites/default/files/files/Veterans_Report_FINAL.pdf.

[65] SBA, *Fiscal Year 2010 Congressional Budget Justification*, p. 30, at http://www.sba.gov/sites/default/files/Congressional_Budget_Justification_2010.pdf. Also see no credit elsewhere clause in P.L. 83-163, the Small Business Act (as amended).

[66] SBA, "SBA Lending Statistics for Major Programs (as of 9/30/2014)," at http://www.sba.gov/sites/default/files/aboutsbaarticle/WebsiteReport_asof9_30_2014.pdf.

buildings; acquire (by purchase or lease) and install fixed assets; purchase inventory, supplies, and raw materials; finance working capital; and refinance certain outstanding debts. The 7(a) program's loan maturity for working capital, machinery, and equipment (not to exceed the life of the equipment) is typically 5 years to 10 years, and the loan maturity for real estate is up to 25 years. Interest rates are negotiated between the borrower and lender but are subject to maximum rates.[67]

In FY2014, the SBA approved 52,044 7(a) loans totaling $19.19 billion, including 2,113 loans to veterans (4.1%) totaling $597.96 million (3.1%). In FY2014, the average approved 7(a) loan amount to a veteran was $282,992.[68]

The SBA's 504/CDC loan guaranty program is administered through nonprofit certified development companies (CDCs). It provides long-term fixed rate financing for major fixed assets, such as land, buildings, equipment, and machinery. Of the total project costs, a third-party lender must provide at least 50% of the financing, the CDC provides up to 40% of the financing through a 100% SBA-guaranteed debenture, and the applicant provides at least 10% of the financing. The 504/CDC program's name is derived from Section 504 of the Small Business Investment Act of 1958 (P.L. 85-699, as amended), which provides the most recent authorization for the sale of 504/CDC debentures.[69] In FY2014, the average approved 504/CDC loan amount was $713,582.[70]

In FY2014, the SBA approved 5,885 504/CDC loans totaling $4.2 billion, including 263 loans to veterans (4.4%) totaling $168.1 million (4.0%). In FY2014, the average approved 504/CDC loan amount to a veteran was $639,216.[71]

The SBA also administers several 7(a) loan guaranty subprograms that offer streamlined and expedited loan procedures to encourage lenders to provide loans to specific groups of borrowers identified by the SBA as having difficulty accessing capital. In the past, the Patriot Express program (2007-2013) encouraged lenders to provide loans to veterans and their spouses. It provided loans of up to $500,000 (with a guaranty of up to 85% of loans of $150,000 or less and up to 75% of loans exceeding $150,000).[72]

---

[67] For further information and analysis concerning the SBA's 7(a) loan guaranty program, see CRS Report R41146, *Small Business Administration 7(a) Loan Guaranty Program*, by Robert Jay Dilger.

[68] SBA, "SBA Lending Statistics for Major Programs (as of 9/30/2014)," at http://www.sba.gov/sites/default/files/aboutsbaarticle/WebsiteReport_asof9_30_2014.pdf.

[69] For further information and analysis concerning the SBA's 504 Certified Development Company (504/CDC) loan guaranty program, see CRS Report R41184, *Small Business Administration 504/CDC Loan Guaranty Program*, by Robert Jay Dilger.

[70] SBA, "SBA Lending Statistics for Major Programs (as of 9/30/2014)," at http://www.sba.gov/sites/default/files/aboutsbaarticle/WebsiteReport_asof9_30_2014.pdf.

[71] Ibid.

[72] Eligible businesses were required to be owned and controlled (51% or more) by one or more of the following groups: veteran, active duty military participating in the military's Transition Assistance Program, reservist or national guard member or a spouse of any of these groups, a widowed spouse of a servicemember who died while in service, or a widowed spouse of a veteran who died of a service-connected disability. See SBA, "SOP 50 10 5(E): Lender and Development Company Loan Programs," (effective June 1, 2012), pp. 83, 127, at http://www.sba.gov/sites/default/files/SOP%2050%2010%205(E)%20(5-16-2012)%20clean.pdf. The program's interest rates were negotiable with the lender, subject to the same maximum rate limitations as the 7(a) program, which vary depending upon the size and maturity of the loan. It also had the same fees as the 7(a) program, which also vary depending on the size and maturity of the loan.

The SBA considered the Patriot Express program a success, but some veterans' organizations expressed concern that many veterans, especially during and immediately following the Great Recession (December 2007 to June 2009), experienced difficulty finding lenders willing to provide them Patriot Express loans.[73] In addition, GAO reported in September 2013 that with the exception of loans approved in 2007, Patriot Express loans defaulted at a higher rate than regular 7(a) loans and loans made under the SBAExpress program (a 7(a) loan guaranty subprogram offering streamlined borrower application and lender approval procedures).[74] Over its history, the Patriot Express program disbursed 9,414 loans totaling more than $791 million.[75]

On January 1, 2014, the SBA implemented a new, streamlined application process for 7(a) loans of $350,000 or less. As part of an overall effort to streamline and simplify its loan application process, the SBA also eliminated several 7(a) subprograms, including the Patriot Express program. In anticipation of ending the Patriot Express program, the SBA announced on November 8, 2013, that it would waive the up-front, one-time loan guaranty fee for all veteran loans under the SBAExpress program from January 1, 2014, through the end of FY2014 (called the Veterans Advantage Program).[76]

The SBA announced that the fee waiver was part "of SBA's broader efforts to make sure that veterans have the tools they need to start and grow a business."[77] The Obama Administration has continued this fee waiver for veterans through the end of FY2015, and legislation has been introduced (S. 2143, the Veterans Entrepreneurship Act) to make the fee waiver permanent.

---

[73] U.S. Congress, Senate Committee on Small Business and Entrepreneurship, *Assessing Federal Small Business Assistance Programs for Veterans and Reservists*, hearing, 110th Cong., 1st sess., January 31, 2007, S.Hrg. 110-209 (Washington: GPO, 2007), p. 32; U.S. Congress, House Committee on Veterans' Affairs, Subcommittee on Economic Opportunity, *Status of Veterans Small Business*, hearing, 111th Cong., 2nd sess., April 29, 2010, House Committee on Veterans' Affairs Serial No. 111-74 (Washington: GPO, 2010), pp. 17, 75; SBA, "Popular SBA Patriot Express Loan Initiative Renewed for Three More Years," December 10, 2010, at http://www.sba.gov/content/popular-sba-patriot-express-loan-initiative-renewed-three-more-years; and U.S. Congress, House Committee on Veterans' Affairs, Subcommittee on Economic Opportunity, *Status of Veterans Small Business*, hearing, 111th Cong., 2nd sess., April 29, 2010, House Committee on Veterans' Affairs Serial No. 111-74 (Washington: GPO, 2010), p. 17.

[74] GAO, *Patriot Express: SBA Should Evaluate the Program and Enhance Eligibility Controls*, GA)-13-727, September 13, 2013, pp. i, 10, 16-20, 25-30, 46-49, at http://www.gao.gov/assets/660/657793.pdf.

[75] SBA, Office of Congressional and Legislative Affairs, correspondence with the author, February 21, 2014.

[76] The SBAExpress program's fees are the same as the 7(a) loan program's fees. SBAExpress loans of $150,000 or less approved in FY2014 do not have an up-front, one-time loan guaranty fee, and these loans do not have an annual, ongoing loan servicing fee. SBAExpress loans of $150,001 to the SBAExpress limit of $350,000, with a maturity of one year or less, have a 0.25% up-front, one-time loan guaranty fee and a 0.52% annual, ongoing loan servicing fee. SBAExpress loans of $150,001 to the SBAExpress limit of $350,000, with a maturity over one year have a 3.0% up-front, one-time loan guaranty fee and a 0.52% annual, ongoing loan servicing fee. To qualify for a waiver of the 3.0% up-front, one-time loan guaranty fee, the business must be 51% or more owned and controlled by an individual or individuals in one or more of the following groups: veterans (other than dishonorably discharged); service-disabled veterans; active duty military servicemembers participating in the military's Transition Assistance Program (TAP); reservists and National Guard members; current spouse of any veteran, active duty servicemember, or any reservist or National Guard member; or widowed spouse of a servicemember who died while in service or of a service-connected disability. See SBA, "SBA Announces New Measures to Help Get Small Business Loans Into the Hands of Veterans," November 8, 2013, at http://www.sba.gov/content/sba-announces-new-measures-help-get-small-business-loans-hands-veterans; and SBA, "Procedural Notice: SBA Veterans Advantage," December 18, 2013, at http://www.sba.gov/sites/default/files/5000-1299.pdf.

[77] SBA, "SBA Announces New Measures to Help Get Small Business Loans Into the Hands of Veterans," November 8, 2013, at http://www.sba.gov/content/sba-announces-new-measures-help-get-small-business-loans-hands-veterans.

The SBAExpress program is designed to increase the availability of credit to small businesses by permitting lenders to use their existing documentation and procedures in return for receiving a reduced SBA guaranty on loans.[78] It provides a 50% loan guaranty on loan amounts up to $350,000. In FY2014, the SBA approved 26,545 SBAExpress loans (51.0% of total 7(a) program loan approvals) totaling $1.91 billion (9.9% of total 7(a) program amount approvals).[79]

In FY2014, the SBA also waived the up-front, one-time loan guaranty fee and the annual, ongoing servicing fee for all 7(a) loans of $150,000 or less. The Obama Administration has continued these fee waivers through the end of FY2015. In addition, "to encourage lending to veteran-owned small businesses" the Administration is waiving 50% of the up-front, one-time loan guaranty fee on all non-SBAExpress 7(a) loans to veterans exceeding $150,000 in FY2015.[80]

Congressional Issues: Access

As mentioned previously, the SBA has indicated in both testimony at congressional hearings and in press releases that it views the Patriot Express program and its own overall effort to enhance veterans' access to capital as a success.[81] For example, when the SBA announced its veterans' fee waiver for the SBAExpress program, it also announced that its lending to veteran-owned small businesses had nearly doubled since 2009 and that "in FY 2013, SBA supported $1.86 billion in loans for 3,094 veteran-owned small businesses."[82]

Congressional testimony provided by various veteran service organizations provides a somewhat different perspective. The SBA's self-evaluation of its success in assisting veterans access capital has focused primarily on the agency's efforts to streamline the loan application approval process (e.g., minimizing paperwork requirements and reducing the time necessary for the SBA to review and approve applications submitted by local lenders) and aggregate lending amounts (e.g., the number and amount of loans approved). In contrast, veteran service organizations focus primarily on program outcomes, especially the likelihood of a veteran being approved for a SBA loan by a local lender. For example, a representative of the American Legion testified at a congressional hearing in 2010 that, at that time, being turned down for a SBA Patriot Express loan by a private lender "is probably the largest, most frequent complaint that we receive from our business owners."[83] At that same congressional hearing, a representative of the Vietnam Veterans of America testified in response to that statement that "I would have to concur … in talking with some of the veterans with regard to the Patriot Express Loan, they are having difficulties also to

---

[78] SBA, "The SBA Express Pilot Program: Inspection Report," June 1998, p. 3, at http://archive.sba.gov/idc/groups/public/documents/sba/oig_loarchive_980601.pdf.

[79] SBA, "SBA Lending Statistics for Major Programs (as of 9/30/2014)," at http://www.sba.gov/sites/default/files/aboutsbaarticle/WebsiteReport_asof9_30_2014.pdf.

[80] SBA, "SBA Information Notice: SBA Veterans Advantage – Renewal and Expansion of Fee Relief," September 19, 2014, at http://www.sba.gov/sites/default/files/lender_notices/5000-1319.pdf.

[81] U.S. Congress, House Committee on Veterans' Affairs, Subcommittee on Economic Opportunity, *Status of Veterans Small Business*, hearing, 111th Cong., 2nd sess., April 29, 2010, House Committee on Veterans' Affairs Serial No. 111-74 (Washington: GPO, 2010), p. 75.

[82] SBA, "SBA Announces New Measures to Help Get Small Business Loans Into the Hands of Veterans," November 8, 2013, at http://www.sba.gov/content/sba-announces-new-measures-help-get-small-business-loans-hands-veterans.

[83] U.S. Congress, House Committee on Veterans' Affairs, Subcommittee on Economic Opportunity, *Status of Veterans Small Business*, hearing, 111th Cong., 2nd sess., April 29, 2010, House Committee on Veterans' Affairs Serial No. 111-74 (Washington: GPO, 2010), p. 17.

---

acquire that capital. The rationale seems to be … the banks in general seem to be tightening the credit, their lending practices, so that is … what we are hearing."[84] More recently, GAO reported in 2013 that "selected loan recipients, lenders, and veteran service organizations said that a low awareness of the Patriot Express program among the military community was among the most frequently cited challenges."[85]

No empirical assessments of veterans' experiences with either the SBA's Patriot Express or SBAExpress loan programs exist that would be useful for determining the relative ease or difficulty for veteran-owned small business owners of accessing capital through the SBA's loan programs. Since 2010, many lenders report that they have eased their credit standards, at least somewhat, for small business loans, suggesting the experiences of veterans seeking a SBA loan guaranty today may be improved compared with their experiences in 2010. However, GAO found in 2013 that many veterans were not fully aware of the SBA's Patriot Express program and that "over half of the Patriot Express loan recipients, six of the eight lenders, and two veteran service organizations … said that [the] SBA could do more to increase outreach to veteran entrepreneurs and better market the program to the military community."[86] GAO reported that low awareness of the SBA's Patriot Express program and the SBA's participating lenders were a continuing challenge for the SBA.[87]

One option to provide additional information concerning veterans' experiences with the SBA's lenders would be to survey veterans who have received a SBA guaranteed loan. The survey could include questions concerning these veterans' views of the programs, including the application process. However, obtaining a comprehensive list of veterans to survey who have been turned down for a SBA guaranteed loan by a private lender would be difficult given privacy concerns.

Federal Contracting Goals for Service-Disabled Veteran-Owned Small Businesses

Since 1978, federal agency heads have been required to establish federal procurement contracting goals, in consultation with the SBA, "that realistically reflect the potential of small business concerns" to participate in federal procurement. Each agency is required, at the conclusion of each fiscal year, to report its progress in meeting the goals to the SBA.[88] The SBA negotiates the goals with each federal agency and establishes a *small business eligible* baseline for evaluating the agency's performance.

The small business eligible baseline excludes certain contracts that the SBA has determined do not realistically reflect the potential for small business participation in federal procurement, such as contracts awarded to mandatory and directed sources, awarded and performed overseas, funded predominately from agency-generated sources, not covered by Federal Acquisition Regulations, and not reported in the Federal Procurement Data System (e.g., contracts or government

---

[84] Ibid.

[85] GAO, *Patriot Express: SBA Should Evaluate the Program and Enhance Eligibility Controls*, GA)-13-727, September 13, 2013, p. 33, at http://www.gao.gov/assets/660/657793.pdf.

[86] Ibid.

[87] Ibid.

[88] P.L. 95-507, a bill to amend the Small Business Act and the Small Business Investment Act of 1958.

procurement card purchases valued less than \$3,000).[89] These exclusions typically account for 18% to 20% of all federal prime contracts each year.

The SBA then evaluates the agencies' performance against their negotiated goals annually, using data from the Federal Procurement Data System–Next Generation, managed by the U.S. General Services Administration, to generate the small business eligible baseline. This information is compiled into the official Small Business Goaling Report, which the SBA releases annually.

Over the years, federal government-wide procurement contracting goals have been established for small businesses generally (P.L. 100-656, the Business Opportunity Development Reform Act of 1988, and P.L. 105-135, the HUBZone Act of 1997—Title VI of the Small Business Reauthorization Act of 1997); small businesses owned and controlled by socially and economically disadvantaged individuals (P.L. 100-656, the Business Opportunity Development Reform Act of 1988); women (P.L. 103-355, the Federal Acquisition Streamlining Act of 1994); small businesses located within a Historically Underutilized Business Zone, or HUBZone (P.L. 105-135, the HUBZone Act of 1997—Title VI of the Small Business Reauthorization Act of 1997); and small businesses owned and controlled by a service-disabled veteran (P.L. 106-50, the Veterans Entrepreneurship and Small Business Development Act of 1999).

The current federal small business contracting goals are

- at least 23% of the total value of all small business eligible prime contract awards to small businesses for each fiscal year;

- 5% of the total value of all small business eligible prime contract awards and subcontract awards to small disadvantaged businesses for each fiscal year;

- 5% of the total value of all small business eligible prime contract awards and subcontract awards to women-owned small businesses;

- 3% of the total value of all small business eligible prime contract awards and subcontract awards to HUBZone small businesses; and

- 3% of the total value of all small business eligible prime contract awards and subcontract awards to service-disabled veteran-owned small businesses.[90]

There are no punitive consequences for not meeting the small business procurement goals. However, the SBA's Small Business Goaling Report is distributed widely, receives media attention, and heightens public awareness of the issue of small business contracting. For example, agency performance as reported in the SBA's Small Business Goaling Report is often cited by Members during their questioning of federal agency witnesses in congressional hearings.

As shown in **Table 3**, the latest Small Business Goaling Report, using data in the Federal Procurement Data System as of February 19, 2014, indicates that federal agencies met the federal contracting goals for small businesses generally (for the first time in eight years) and for small disadvantaged businesses in FY2013. Federal agencies awarded 23.39% of the value of their small business eligible contracts to small businesses, 8.61% to small disadvantaged businesses,

---

[89] See U.S. General Services Administration, Federal Procurement Data System—Next Generation, "Small Business Goaling Report: Fiscal Year 2013," at https://www.fpds.gov/downloads/top_requests/ FPDSNG_SB_Goaling_FY_2013.pdf.

[90] 15 U.S.C. §644(g)(1)-(2).

4.32% to women-owned small businesses, 1.76% to HUBZone small businesses, and 3.38% to service-disabled veteran-owned small businesses.[91]

For comparative purposes, the table also provides the percentages of total reported federal contracts (without exclusions) awarded to small businesses, small disadvantaged businesses, women-owned small businesses, HUBZone small businesses, and service-disabled veteran-owned small businesses in FY2013.

Table 3. Federal Contracting Goals and Percentage of FY2013 Federal Contract Dollars Awarded to Small Businesses, by Type

Business Type	Federal Goal	Percentage of FY2013 Federal Contracts (small business eligible)	Percentage of FY2013 Federal Contracts (all reported contracts)
Small Businesses	23.0%	23.39%	19.92%
Small Disadvantaged Businesses	5.0%	8.61%	6.97%
Women-Owned Small Businesses	5.0%	4.32%	3.50%
HUBZone Small Businesses	3.0%	1.76%	1.41%
Service-Disabled Veteran-Owned Small Businesses	3.0%	3.38%	2.73%

Source: U.S. Small Business Administration, "Statutory Guidelines," at http://www.sba.gov/content/goaling-guidelines-0 (federal goals); U.S. General Services Administration, Federal Procurement Data System—Next Generation, "Small Business Goaling Report: Fiscal Year 2013," at https://www.fpds.gov/downloads/top_requests/FPDSNG_SB_Goaling_FY_2013.pdf ; and U.S. General Services Administration, Federal Procurement Data System—Next Generation, at https://www.fpds.gov/fpdsng/ (contract dollars).

Notes: The Federal Procurement Data System (FPDS) is a dynamic system with records updated daily. The FY 2013 Small Business Goaling Report is based on FPDS data as of February 19, 2014. It reports that small business eligible contracts at that time totaled $355.4 billion and that $83.1 billion was awarded to small businesses, $30.6 billion to small disadvantaged businesses, $15.4 billion to women-owned small businesses, $6.2 billion to SBA-certified HUBZone small businesses, and $12.0 billion to service-disabled veteran-owned small businesses. The Small Business Goaling Report for FY2013 does not indicate the total amount of federal contracts reported in the FPDS as of February 19, 2014. Therefore, the percentages provided in the column for all reported contracts were calculated using FPDS data as reported on September 23, 2014: $462.0 billion in total contracts, $92.0 billion awarded to small businesses, $32.2 billion to small disadvantaged businesses, $16.2 billion to women-owned small businesses, $6.5 billion to HUBZone small businesses, and $12.6 billion to service-disabled veteran-owned small businesses.

---

[91] U.S. General Services Administration, Federal Procurement Data System—Next Generation, "Small Business Goaling Report: Fiscal Year 2013," at https://www.fpds.gov/downloads/top_requests/FPDSNG_SB_Goaling_FY_2013.pdf.

Congressional Issues: Contracting Fraud[92]

The prevention of fraud in federal small business contracting programs, and in the SBA's loan programs as well, has been a priority for both Congress and the SBA for many years, primarily because reports of fraud in these programs emerge with some regularity.[93] Of particular interest to veterans, GAO has found that "the lack of an effective government-wide fraud-prevention program" has left the service-disabled veteran-owned small business program "vulnerable to fraud and abuse."[94]

Under the Small Business Act, a small business owned and controlled by a service-disabled veteran can qualify for a federal government procurement set-aside (a procurement in which only certain businesses may compete) or a sole-source award (awards proposed or made after soliciting and negotiating with only one source) if the small business is at least 51% unconditionally and directly owned and controlled by one or more service-disabled veteran.[95] A veteran is defined as a person who has served "in the active military, naval, or air service, and who was discharged or released under conditions other than dishonorable."[96] A disability is service related when it "was incurred or aggravated ... in [the] line of duty in the active military, naval, or air service."[97]

Federal agencies may set aside procurements for service-disabled veteran-owned small businesses only if the contracting officer reasonably expects that offers will be received from at least two responsible small businesses and the award will be made at a fair market price (commonly known as the "rule of two" because of the focus on there being at least two small businesses involved).[98]

Federal agencies may award sole contracts to service-disabled veteran-owned small businesses when (1) the contracting officer does not reasonably expect that two or more service-disabled veteran-owned small businesses will submit offers; (2) the anticipated award will not exceed $3.5 million ($6 million for manufacturing contracts); and (3) the award can be made at a fair and reasonable price.[99] Otherwise, sole-source awards may only be made to service-disabled veteran-

---

[92] For additional information and analysis concerning federal procurement small business issues see CRS Report R42981, *Set-Asides for Small Businesses: Legal Requirements and Issues*, by Kate M. Manuel and Erika K. Lunder; and CRS Report R42390, *Federal Contracting and Subcontracting with Small Businesses: Issues in the 112th Congress*, by Kate M. Manuel and Erika K. Lunder.

[93] For example, see GAO, *Small Business Administration: Undercover Tests Show HUBZone Program Remains Vulnerable to Fraud and Abuse*, GAO-10-920T, July 28, 2010, at http://www.gao.gov/assets/130/125130.pdf; GAO, *8(a) Program: Fourteen Ineligible Firms Received $325 Million in Sole-Source and Set-Aside Contracts*, GAO-10-425, March 30, 2010, at http://www.gao.gov/assets/310/302472.pdf; GAO, *Service-Disabled Veteran-Owned Small Business Program: Case Studies Show Fraud and Abuse Allowed Ineligible Firms to Obtain Millions of Dollars in Contracts*, GAO-10-108, October 23, 2009, at http://www.gao.gov/products/GAO-10-108; and GAO, *Service-Disabled Veteran-Owned Small Business Program: Vulnerability to Fraud and Abuse Remains*, GAO-12-697, August 1, 2012, at http://www.gao.gov/assets/600/593238.pdf.

[94] GAO, *Service-Disabled Veteran-Owned Small Business Program: Preliminary Information on Actions Taken by Agencies to Address Fraud and Abuse and Remaining Vulnerabilities*, GAO-11-589T, July 28, 2011, p. 3, at http://www.gao.gov/products/GAO-11-589T.

[95] 15 U.S.C. §632(q)(1) & (4); P.L. 108-183, the Veterans Benefits Act of 2003; and P.L. 109-461, the Veterans Benefits, Health Care, and Information Technology Act of 2006.

[96] 38 U.S.C. §101(2).

[97] 38 U.S.C. §101(16).

[98] 15 U.S.C. §657f(b).

[99] 15 U.S.C. §657f(a)(1)-(3) (statutory requirements); and 48 C.F.R. §19.1406(a) (increasing the price thresholds).

---

owned small businesses under other authority, such as the Competition in Contracting Act.[100] Service-disabled veteran-owned small businesses are not eligible for price evaluation preferences in unrestricted competitions.

In addition, the Department of Veterans Affairs (VA) is statutorily required to establish annual goals for the awarding of VA contracts to both service-disabled veteran-owned small businesses and small businesses owned by other veterans.[101] The VA is authorized to use "other than competitive procedures" in meeting these goals. For example, it may award any contract whose value is below the simplified acquisition threshold (generally $150,000) to a veteran-owned business on a sole-source basis, and it may also make sole-source awards of contracts whose value (including options) is between $150,000 and $5 million, provided that certain conditions are met. When these conditions are not met, the VA is generally required to set aside the contract for service-disabled or other veteran-owned small businesses.[102]

Service-disabled veteran-owned small businesses can generally self-certify as to their eligibility for contracting preferences available under the Small Business Act.[103] However, in an effort to address fraud in VA contracting, veteran-owned and service-disabled veteran-owned small businesses must be listed in the VA's VetBiz database and have their eligibility verified by the VA to be eligible for preferences in certain VA contracts.[104]

Firms that fraudulently misrepresent their size or status have long been subject to civil and criminal penalties under Section 16 of the Small Business Act; SBA regulations implementing Section 16; and other provisions of law, such as the False Claims Act, Fraud and False Statements Act, Program Fraud Civil Remedies Act, and Contract Disputes Act.[105]

Several bills were introduced during the 112th Congress to address fraud in small business contracting programs in various ways. Of particular interest to veterans, S. 3572, the Restoring Tax and Regulatory Certainty to Small Businesses Act of 2012, and S. 633, the Small Business Contracting Fraud Prevention Act of 2011, would have, among other changes, amended Section 16 of the Small Business Act to expressly include service-disabled veteran-owned small

---

[100] 10 U.S.C. §2304(c)(1)-(7) (procurements of defense agencies); and 41 U.S.C. §3304(a)(1)-(7) (procurements of civilian agencies). *See also* 48 C.F.R. §§6.302-1 to 6.302-7; and CRS Report R40516, *Competition in Federal Contracting: A Legal Overview*, by Kate M. Manuel.

[101] P.L. 109-461. the Veterans Benefits, Health Care, and Information Technology Act of 2006; and P.L. 110-389, the Veterans' Benefits Improvements Act of 2008.

[102] For further information and analysis of federal contracting legal authorities generally and affecting the Department of Veterans Affairs, see CRS Report R42391, *Legal Authorities Governing Federal Contracting and Subcontracting with Small Businesses*, by Kate M. Manuel and Erika K. Lunder http://www.crs.gov/pages/Reports.aspx? PRODCODE=R42391

[103] 13 C.F.R. §125.15.

[104] 38 U.S.C. §8127(a)(1)(A). P.L. 109-461, the Veterans Benefits, Health Care, and Information Technology Act of 2006, requires the Secretary of Veterans Affairs to "establish a goal for each fiscal year for participation in Department contracts (including subcontracts)" by veteran-owned small businesses. The Secretary is also required to establish a separate goal for the participation of service-disabled veteran-owned small businesses in agency contracts and subcontracts. 38 U.S.C. §8127(a)(1)(A). However, the latter goal can be no less than the government-wide goal for the percentage of contract and subcontract dollars awarded to service-disabled veteran-owned small businesses given in Section 15(g)(1) of the Small Business Act (currently 3%), while the former goal is within the Secretary's discretion. *See* 38 U.S.C. §8127(a)(2)-(3).

[105] See 15 U.S.C. §645; and 13 C.F.R. §125.29.

---

businesses among the types of small businesses subject to penalties for fraud under that section.[106] The bills would also have required service-disabled veteran-owned small businesses to register in the VA's VetBiz database, or any successor database, and have their status verified by the VA to be eligible for contracting preferences for service-disabled veteran-owned small businesses under the Small Business Act.

In addition, during the 113th Congress, S. 2334, the Improving Opportunities for Service-Disabled Veteran-Owned Small Businesses Act of 2013, and its companion bill in the House, H.R. 2882, and H.R. 4435, the Howard P. "Buck" McKeon National Defense Authorization Act for Fiscal Year 2015, which was passed by the House on May 22, 2014, include a provision authorizing the transfer of the VetBiz database's administration and the verification of service-disabled veteran owned small businesses from the VA to the SBA.

Advocates of requiring service-disabled veteran-owned small businesses to register in the VetBiz database and have their status verified by the VA (or the SBA) to be eligible for contracting preferences under the Small Business Act argue that doing so would reduce fraud.[107] As then-Senator Snowe stated on the Senate floor when she introduced S. 633, "Our legislation attempts to remedy the spate of illegitimate firms siphoning away contracts from the rightful businesses trying to compete within the SBA's contracting programs."[108]

Others worry that requiring service-disabled veteran-owned small businesses to register in the VetBiz database and have their status verified by the VA (or the SBA) to be eligible for contracting preferences under the Small Business Act may add to the paperwork burdens of small businesses. They seek alternative ways to address the need to reduce fraud in federal small business procurement programs that do not increase the paperwork requirements of small businesses.[109] Still others note that the effectiveness of any change to prevent fraud in veteran-owned and service-disabled veteran-owned small business procurement programs largely depends upon how the change is implemented. For example, in July 2011, the VA's Office of Inspector General concluded that the VA's implementation of its veteran-owned and service-disabled veteran-owned small business procurement fraud prevention programs needed improvement:

> We project that VA awarded ineligible businesses at least 1,400 VOSB [Veteran Owned Small Business] and SDVOSB [Service-Disabled Veteran Owned Small Business] contracts valued at $500 million annually and that it will award about $2.5 billion in VOSB and SDVOSB contracts to ineligible businesses over the next 5 years if it does not strengthen oversight and verification procedures. VA and the Office of Small and Disadvantaged

---

[106] Currently, Section 36 of the Small Business Act, which governs set-asides and sole-source awards for service-disabled veteran-owned small businesses, provides that "[r]ules similar to the rules of paragraphs (5) and (6) of Section 637(m) of this title shall apply for purposes of this section." Section 8(m) governs set-asides for women-owned small businesses and itself provides that such businesses are subject to penalties for fraud under Section 16. Thus, an argument could potentially be made that service-disabled veteran-owned small businesses are currently subject to penalties under Section 16 even if they are not expressly included there. See CRS Report R42390, *Federal Contracting and Subcontracting with Small Businesses: Issues in the 112th Congress*, by Kate M. Manuel and Erika K. Lunder.

[107] See 13 C.F.R. §§125.9-125.13.

[108] Senator Olympia Snowe, "Statements on Introduced Bills and Joint Resolutions," remarks in the Senate, *Congressional Record*, vol. 157, part no. 41 (March 17, 2011), p. S1843.

[109] U.S. Congress, House Committee on Oversight and Government Reform, Subcommittee on Technology, Information Policy, Intergovernmental Relations and Procurement Reform, *Jobs for Wounded Warriors: Increasing Access to Contracts for Service Disabled Veterans*, 112th Cong., 2nd sess., February 7, 2012, Serial No. 112-143 (Washington: GPO, 2012), pp. 86-90.

Business Utilization (OSDBU) need to improve contracting officer oversight, document reviews, completion of site visits for "high-risk" businesses, and the accuracy of VetBiz Vendor Information Pages information.[110]

For further information and analysis concerning legislation designed to address fraud in small business contracting programs, see CRS Report R42390, *Federal Contracting and Subcontracting with Small Businesses: Issues in the 112th Congress*, by Kate M. Manuel and Erika K. Lunder.

The Military Reservist Economic Injury Disaster Loan Program

P.L. 106-50, the Veterans Entrepreneurship and Small Business Development Act of 1999, signed into law on August 17, 1999, authorized the SBA's Military Reservist Economic Injury Disaster Loan (MREIDL) program. The SBA published the final rule establishing the program in the *Federal Register* on July 25, 2001, with an effective date of August 24, 2001.[111]

The Senate Committee on Small Business provided, in its committee report on the Veterans Entrepreneurship and Small Business Development Act of 1999, the following reasons for supporting the authorization of the MREIDL Program:

> During and after the Persian Gulf War in the early 1990's, the Committee heard from reservists whose businesses were harmed, severely crippled, or even lost, by their absence. Problems faced by reservists called to active duty and their small businesses were of a varied nature and included cash-flow problems, difficulties with training an appropriate alternate manager on very short notice to run the business during the period of service, lost clientele upon return, and on occasion, bankruptcy. These hardships can occur during a period of national emergency or during a period of contingency operation when troops are deployed overseas.
>
> To help such reservists and their small businesses, the Committee seeks to provide credit and management assistance to small businesses when an essential employee (i.e., an owner, manager or vital member of the business' staff) is a reservist called to active duty. The Committee believes that financial assistance in the form of loans, loan deferrals and managerial guidance are effective ways to minimize the adverse financial demands of the call to active duty. They not only ameliorate financial difficulties but also strengthen small businesses.[112]

---

[110] U.S. Department of Veterans Affairs, Office of Inspector General, "Audit of Veteran-Owned and Service-Disabled Veteran-Owned Small Business Programs," July 25, 2011, p. i, at http://www.va.gov/oig/52/reports/2011/VAOIG-10-02436-234.pdf.

[111] SBA, "Military Reservist Economic Injury Disaster Loans," 66 *Federal Register* 38528-38531, July 25, 2001.

[112] U.S. Congress, Senate Committee on Small Business, *Veterans Entrepreneurship and Small Business Development Act of 1999*, report to accompany H.R. 1568, 106th Cong., 1st sess., August 4, 1999, S.Rept. 106-136 (Washington: GPO, 1999), p. 4.

The House Committee on Small Business also supported the program's authorization, indicating in its committee report that the program

> will also fulfill a long unmet need to assist our military reservists who are small business owners. Often these individuals, called to service at short notice, come back from fighting to protect our freedoms only to find their businesses in shambles. H.R. 1568 will establish loan deferrals, technical and managerial assistance, and loan programs for these citizen soldiers so that while they risk their lives they need not risk their livelihoods.[113]

As mentioned previously, the SBA provides direct loans for owners of businesses of all sizes, homeowners, and renters to assist their recovery from natural disasters. The SBA's MREIDL program provides disaster assistance in the form of direct loans of up to $2 million to help small business owners who are not able to obtain credit elsewhere to (1) meet ordinary and necessary operating expenses that they could have met but are not able to meet; or (2) enable them to market, produce, or provide products or services ordinarily marketed, produced, or provided by the business that cannot be done because an essential employee has been called up to active duty in his or her role as a military reservist or member of the National Guard due to a period of military conflict.[114] Under specified circumstances, the SBA may waive the $2 million limit (e.g., the small business is in immediate danger of going out of business, is a major source of employment, employs 10% or more of the workforce within the commuting area in which the business is located).[115]

P.L. 106-50 defines an essential employee as "an individual who is employed by a small business concern and whose managerial or technical expertise is critical to the successful day-to-day operations of that small business concern."[116] The act defines a military conflict as (1) a period of war declared by Congress; or (2) a period of national emergency declared by Congress or the President; or (3) a period of contingency operation. A contingency operation is designated by the Secretary of Defense as an operation in which our military may become involved in military actions, operations, or hostilities (peacekeeping operations).[117]

The SBA is authorized to make such disaster loans either directly or in cooperation with banks or other lending institutions through agreements to participate on an immediate or deferred basis. The loan term may be up to a maximum of 30 years and is determined by the SBA in accordance with the borrower's ability to repay the loan. The loan's interest rate is the SBA's published interest rate for an Economic Injury Disaster Loan at the time the application for assistance is approved by the SBA. Economic Injury Disaster Loan interest rates may not exceed 4%.

---

[113] Ibid., p. 15.

[114] SBA, "Disaster Assistance Program: SOP 50-30-7," May 13, 2011, p. 48, at http://www.sba.gov/sites/default/files/SOP%2050%2030%207.pdf; and 13 C.F.R. §123.508. For further information and analysis concerning the SBA's disaster assistance loan program see CRS Report R41309, *The SBA Disaster Loan Program: Overview and Possible Issues for Congress*, by Bruce R. Lindsay.

[115] 13 C.F.R. §123.507.

[116] P.L. 106-50, the Veterans Entrepreneurship and Small Business Development Act of 1999, Section 402. Assistance To Active Duty Military Reservists; and 15 U.S.C. §636(b). The SBA's Military Reservist Economic Injury Disaster Loan Program applies to economic injury suffered or likely to be suffered as the result of a period of military conflict occurring or ending on or after March 24, 1999.

[117] P.L. 106-50, the Veterans Entrepreneurship and Small Business Development Act of 1999, Section 402. Assistance To Active Duty Military Reservists; and 15 U.S.C. §636(c).

The SBA is not required by law to require collateral on disaster loans. However, the SBA has established collateral requirements for disaster loans based on "a balance between protection of the Agency's interest as a creditor and as a provider of disaster assistance."[118] The SBA generally does not require collateral to secure a MREIDL loan of $50,000 or less. Larger loan amounts require collateral, but the SBA will not decline a request for a MREIDL loan for a lack of collateral if the SBA is reasonably certain the borrower can repay the loan.[119]

In FY2013, the SBA disbursed three MREIDL loans amounting to $121,200. Since the MREIDL's inception through September 30, 2013, the SBA has disbursed 344 MREIDL loans amounting to $32.35 million. Of these 344 loans, 70 loans (20.3% of the total number of MREIDL loans disbursed), amounting to $7.32 million (22.6% of the total amount of MREIDL loans disbursed), have been charged off (a declaration that the debt is unlikely to be collected) by the SBA.[120]

Because the MREIDL program is relatively small and noncontroversial, this report does not present a discussion of the congressional issues affecting the program.

Concluding Observations

Congressional interest in federal programs designed to assist veterans in their transitions from military into civilian life has increased in recent years for a variety of reasons, especially because of the relatively high rate of unemployment experienced by veterans who have left the military since 2001. The SBA's veteran assistance programs have also experienced a heightened level of congressional interest and scrutiny in recent Congresses. For example, the SBA's veteran business development programs, loan guaranty programs, and federal procurement programs for small businesses generally, including service-disabled veteran-owned small businesses, have all been subject to congressional hearings during the past two Congresses. Also, as has been discussed, several bills have been introduced in recent Congresses to address the SBA's management of these programs and fraud.

Given the many factors that influence business success, measuring the effectiveness of the SBA's veteran assistance programs, especially the programs' effect on veteran job retention and creation, is both complicated and challenging. For example, it is difficult to determine with any degree of precision or certainty the extent to which any changes in the success of a small business result primarily from that business's participation in the SBA's programs or from changes in the broader economy. That task is made even more challenging by the absence of performance outcome measures that could serve as a guide. In most instances, the SBA uses program performance measures that focus on indicators that are primarily output related, such as the number and amount of loans approved for veteran-owned small businesses and the number and amount of federal contracts awarded to service-disabled veteran-owned small businesses.

---

[118] SBA, "Disaster Assistance Program: SOP 50-30-7," May 13, 2011, p. 152, at http://www.sba.gov/sites/default/files/ SOP%2050%2030%207.pdf.

[119] 13 C.F.R. §123.513.

[120] SBA, Office of Congressional and Legislative Affairs, "Correspondence with Robert Dilger," January 16, 2014. In FY2011, the SBA disbursed 10 MREIDL loans amounting to $1.15 million. In FY2012, the SBA disbursed seven MREIDL loans amounting to $834,300.

Both GAO and the SBA's Office of Inspector General have recommended that the SBA adopt more outcome-related performance measures for the SBA's loan guaranty programs, such as tracking the number of borrowers that remain in business after receiving a SBA guaranteed loan to measure the extent to which the SBA contributed to their ability to stay in business.[121] Other performance-oriented measures that Congress might also consider include requiring the SBA to survey veterans who participate in its business development programs or who have received a SBA guaranteed loan. This survey could provide information related to the difficulty the veterans experienced in obtaining a loan from the private sector, their experiences with the SBA's loan application process, and the role the SBA loan had in creating or retaining jobs. The SBA could also survey service-disabled veteran-owned small businesses that were awarded a federal contract to determine the extent to which the SBA was instrumental in their receiving the award and the extent to which the award contributed to their ability to create jobs or expand their scope of operations.

Author Contact Information

Robert Jay Dilger
Senior Specialist in American National Government
rdilger@crs.loc.gov, 7-3110

Sean Lowry
Analyst in Public Finance
slowry@crs.loc.gov, 7-9154

Acknowledgments

The authors would like to express their appreciation to CRS legislative attorneys Kate Manuel and Erika Lunder. Much of this report's section on Congressional Issues: Contracting Fraud was drawn from their work on small business contracting issues, especially CRS Report R42390, *Federal Contracting and Subcontracting with Small Businesses: Issues in the 112th Congress*, by Kate M. Manuel and Erika K. Lunder.

---

[121] GAO, *Small Business Administration: 7(a) Loan Program Needs Additional Performance Measures*, GAO-08-226T, November 1, 2007, p. 2, http://www.gao.gov/new.items/d08226t.pdf; and SBA, Office of the Inspector General, *SBA's Administration of the Microloan Program under the Recovery Act*, December 28, 2009, pp. 6, 7, http://www.gao.gov/new.items/d08226t.pdf.